3/09

ENDANGERED
BATS

Bobbie Kalman & Kristina Lundblad

Crabtree Publishing Company

Earth's Endangered Animals Series
A Bobbie Kalman Book

Dedicated by Kristina Lundblad
For my beautiful and funny friend, Leighton, with love

Editor-in-Chief
Bobbie Kalman

Writing team
Bobbie Kalman
Kristina Lundblad

Substantive editor
Kathryn Smithyman

Editors
Molly Aloian
Robin Johnson
Kelley MacAulay
Rebecca Sjonger

Design
Katherine Kantor
Samantha Crabtree (front cover)

Production coordinator
Heather Fitzpatrick

Photo research
Crystal Foxton

Consultant
Patricia Loesche, Ph.D., Animal Behavior Program,
Department of Psychology, University of Washington

Illustrations
Katherine Kantor: page 19
Cori Marvin: pages 5, 31
Bonna Rouse: back cover, pages 10, 16

Photographs
Animals Animals - Earth Scenes: © Bannister, Anthony: page 31;
    © Dalton, Stephen: page 25 (top); © Shah, Anup: page 9 (bottom)
Bat Conservation International: © Elaine Acker: page 29 (bottom);
    © Jim Kennedy: page 29 (top); © Dan Taylor: page 28; © Merlin D. Tuttle:
    front cover, title page, pages 4, 7 (left), 8, 9 (top), 11, 14, 17, 19, 21, 22, 30
Minden Pictures: Michael & Patricia Fogden: page 3; Claus Meyer: page 12
Naturepl.com: Nick Garbutt: page 23; Hans Christoph Kappel:
    page 25 (bottom); Dietmar Nill: pages 6, 20
Photo Researchers, Inc.: Gregory G. Dimijian, M.D.: page 5;
    Jeff Lepore: page 24; Merlin Tuttle: page 18
Visuals Unlimited: Wendy Dennis: page 15; Rob and Ann Simpson: page 13;
    Richard Thom: page 27
Other images by Corbis and Photodisc

Crabtree Publishing Company

www.crabtreebooks.com   1-800-387-7650

Cataloging-in-Publication Data
Kalman, Bobbie.
    Endangered bats / Bobbie Kalman & Kristina Lundblad.
        p. cm. -- (Earth's endangered animals series)
    Includes index.
    ISBN-13: 978-0-7787-1866-6 (rlb)
    ISBN-10: 0-7787-1866-2 (rlb)
    ISBN-13: 978-0-7787-1912-0 (pbk)
    ISBN-10: 0-7787-1912-X (pbk)
    1. Bats--Juvenile literature. 2. Endangered species--Juvenile literature.
    I. Lundblad, Kristina. II. Title.
    QL737.C5K24 2006
    599.4--dc22
                                                            2005035786
                                                            LC

**Published in
the United States**
PMB 16A
350 Fifth Ave.
Suite 3308
New York, NY
10118

**Published
in Canada**
616 Welland Ave.
St. Catharines, Ontario
Canada
L2M 5V6

**Published in the
United Kingdom**
White Cross Mills
High Town, Lancaster
LA1 4XS
United Kingdom

**Published
in Australia**
386 Mt. Alexander Rd.
Ascot Vale (Melbourne)
VIC 3032

Contents

Endangered bats

There are almost 1,000 **species**, or types, of bats in the world. About one quarter of all bat species are **endangered**. Endangered animals are at risk of dying out in the **wild**, or the areas in which they live that are not controlled by people. If people do not work to protect endangered bats, these animals may soon become **extinct**. Extinct animals no longer live on Earth. Some bat species are already extinct.

Mexican long-nosed bats live in Mexico and in the southern United States. These bats are endangered.

Words to know

Scientists use certain words to describe animals that are in danger. Some of these words are listed below.

vulnerable Describes animals that may become endangered because they face dangers in the wild

endangered Describes animals that are in danger of dying out in the wild

critically endangered Describes animals that are at high risk of dying out in the wild

extinct Describes animals that have died out or animals that have not been seen in the wild for at least 50 years

What are bats?

Bats are **mammals**. Mammals are **warm-blooded** animals. The bodies of warm-blooded animals stay about the same temperatures no matter how hot or cold their surroundings are. All mammals have **backbones**, and most mammals are covered with hair or fur. Baby mammals **nurse**, or drink milk from the bodies of their mothers.

Flying to safety

Bats are the only mammals that can fly. Bats fly to find food and to avoid **predators** on the ground. Raccoons, foxes, snakes, skunks, and **domestic** cats and dogs are all bat predators.

About one quarter of all mammal species are bats!

6

Active at night

Most species of bats, including the black flying fox below, are **nocturnal animals**. Nocturnal animals are active at night. When they are not active, bats rest by hanging upside down. They hang from the walls of caves, from tree branches, and from structures such as houses and bridges.

Hanging around

Bats hang upside down from **perches**, or resting places, that are high above the ground. Resting in high places helps keep bats safe from predators. Bats hang upside down so they can fly away quickly. To begin flying, bats let go of their perches and start flapping their wings. Most bats cannot take off from the ground.

Two groups of bats

Bats are divided into two groups —**microbats** and **megabats**. "Micro" means small. Most species of microbats have tiny bodies. "Mega" means large.

Most megabats have big bodies. Many scientists believe there are about 760 species of microbats and about 170 species of megabats.

Pallid bats are microbats. Pallid bats eat mainly insects that live on the ground, such as katydids, grasshoppers, beetles, and crickets. This pallid bat has caught a katydid.

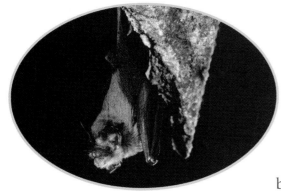

The size of a bumblebee!

The smallest bats belong to a group of microbats called hog-nosed bats. Hog-nosed bats live in Thailand. The **wingspan** of a Kitti's hog-nosed bat is only six inches (15.2 cm)! Kitti's hog-nosed bats are sometimes called bumblebee bats because of their small size.

Flying foxes

Some megabats are called flying foxes because their faces look like the faces of foxes. One of the largest bats in the world is a megabat called Lyle's flying fox. This large bat's wingspan measures almost six feet (1.8 m)! All flying foxes are not as large as the Lyle's flying fox, however. For example, the Rodriguez flying fox, shown right, has a wingspan of about 14 inches (35.6 cm).

Bat body basics

Bats have bodies that are built for flying. Their wings are made up of long arms and fingers, which are covered with a thin layer of skin called a **membrane**. Bats have powerful chest and back muscles, which they use to move their wings. Bats have short legs—their legs are so short that bats rarely walk! Bats use their legs for hanging upside down. They also use their legs to support their wings when they are flying.

Many bats have large ears. Some bats have ears that are unusual in shape. The sizes and shapes of their ears help bats hear well.

Most bat species have black or brown fur. Some bats have bright orange or striped fur, however. Other bat species have almost no fur at all!

Bats have long, sharp claws on their feet. They use their claws to grip their perches.

10

A bat's senses

A bat relies on its five senses—hearing, sight, smell, taste, and touch—to find food and avoid predators. These senses are well developed in all species of bats. Microbats and a few species of megabats have an extra sense called **echolocation**, which is the ability to find objects using sound. As a bat flies, it makes high-pitched sounds. The sounds bounce off the objects they hit and create **echoes**, or waves of sound. In the bat's brain, the echoes create pictures of the objects in the bat's path. Echolocation allows a bat to fly at night without hitting objects such as trees and buildings. The bat knows when any of the objects are **prey**. Prey are animals that predators hunt and eat. The echoes also tell the bat how far away the objects are.

This Townsend's big-eared bat is using echolocation to catch insects that are flying near the water's surface.

Bats around the world

Many bats live in tropical regions, where fruit-producing plants grow year round.

Bats live all over the world. Microbats are far more **widespread** than megabats are. Microbats live on every **continent** except Antarctica, where it is too cold for bats to survive. Megabats live only in Asia, Africa, and Australia. Together, these continents are sometimes called the "Old World." As a result, megabats are also known as "Old World bats."

Some like it hot!

Many species of bats, including all megabats, live in **tropical regions**. Tropical regions are parts of the world where the weather is hot or warm year round.

Temperate regions

Some species of bats live in **temperate regions**, or parts of the world where the seasons change. Most of North America is a temperate region. About 45 species of bats live in North America.

Bat habitats

The natural place where an animal lives is called its **habitat**. Bats live in many habitats, including deserts, forests, and cities. Many bats found in tropical regions live in **rain forests**. A rain forest is a hot forest that receives over 80 inches (203 cm) of rain each year. Scientists believe that there are many species of bats living in rain forests, which have not yet been discovered.

In cold weather, bats huddle together to stay warm.

Resting in the roost

This colony of Indiana bats is resting in its roost.

Bats live in **roosts**. Roosts are shelters where bats rest and hide from predators during daylight hours. Roosts are usually found in areas where bats can find food easily, such as near lakes or in forests.

Colonies

Some bats are **solitary**, which means they live alone. Solitary bats usually roost in trees. Most species of bats live in groups called **colonies**, however. Some colonies are made up of thousands or even millions of bats, whereas others have only a few bats. Large bat colonies need large roosts, which are found in caves, tunnels, abandoned **mines**, and under bridges. Small bat colonies make roosts in hollow parts of trees or under rocks or leaves. Some colonies even make roosts in attics, basements, or sheds!

14

*Many megabat species make **camps**, or outdoor roosts, in treetops. This Madagascar megabat camp stretches across the tops of more than ten trees and includes hundreds of bats!*

15

Growing and changing

As an animal grows, it goes through a set of changes called a **life cycle**. A bat's life cycle begins when the bat is born. The baby bat is called a **pup**.

The pup grows and develops until it is **mature**, or an adult. An adult bat can **mate**, or join together with another adult bat to make babies.

When a pup is born, it begins to nurse immediately. It is furless and helpless until it learns to fly.

A bat grows quickly! Some bat species can reach adult size in only three weeks! Large bat species may take up to ten weeks to reach adult size. A bat is mature when it is between one and three years old.

Most pups can fly by the time they are four weeks old. Once a pup learns how to fly, it stops nursing and begins to find food on its own.

16

Nursery colonies

Most female bats leave their home colonies when they become **pregnant**. They move to **nursery colonies**, where they have babies. A nursery colony is made up of a single species of mother bats and their pups. Most females give birth only to one pup each year. Some nursery colonies are made up of thousands of mothers and pups! Male bats of most species remain with their home colonies and do not help raise the pups.

Huddle up!

When mother bats get hungry, they leave their pups in the roost and fly away to find food. While the mothers are gone, the pups huddle together in tight groups to keep warm.

*A mother gray bat has no trouble finding her pup in a nursery colony. She makes high-pitched sounds to call to her pup, and it replies by squeaking. She also knows her pup by its **scent**, or smell.*

17

What do bats eat?

All megabats are **herbivores**, or animals that eat plant foods. Most megabats eat fruit such as figs, bananas, mangoes, and nuts. Several species of megabats eat plant parts other than fruit.

Some drink **nectar**, which is a sweet liquid found in flowers. Others feed on **pollen**. Pollen is a sticky yellow powder. In order to make seeds, flowers need pollen from other flowers.

Helping plants grow

Bats help plants make seeds by spreading pollen from plant to plant. Moving pollen from one plant to another is called **pollination**. As a bat moves from flower to flower eating nectar or pollen, some pollen sticks to the bat's fur. When the bat moves to other flowers, some of the pollen on the bat's fur rubs off on the flowers.

As the southern long-nosed bat drinks nectar from a saguaro cactus, some pollen may rub off its fur and pollination may take place.

18

Microbats

All microbats are **carnivores**. Carnivores are animals that eat other animals. Most microbats eat insects. Other microbats eat fish, scorpions, lizards, frogs, or birds. Three species of microbats are called vampire bats. Vampire bats drink blood from other animals.

The California leaf-nosed bat eats mainly crickets. It also eats moths and beetles.

We need bats!

Microbats help control insect **populations** by eating thousands of insects each night. Keeping insect populations under control helps people. For example, by eating mosquitoes, bats help keep these insects from biting people.

Bats help farmers by eating insects that destroy **crops**. Big brown bats eat large numbers of insects that feed on crops. Some of the insects that they eat include cucumber beetles, scarab beetles, and stink bugs.

Surviving the cold

Microbats live in places that have cold winters, but insects cannot survive in cold weather. As a result, there are not enough insects for bats to eat during winter. To survive without food, some bats **hibernate**, or go into a deep sleep.

Winter roosts

Bats hibernate in roosts called **hibernacula**. Hibernacula can be found in caves and even in the attics or basements of houses! Bats create hibernacula in places where they will not likely be disturbed.

*This colony of Natterer's bats is in its **hibernaculum**.*

Flying to food

Not all species of bats hibernate during winter. Instead, some bats **migrate**, or move from one place to another for a certain period of time. In autumn, these bats migrate south to warmer areas, where plenty of food is available. In spring, the bats migrate north and return to their home roosts.

In autumn, Mexican free-tailed bats leave their home roosts in southern parts of the United States. They migrate south to Mexico.

21

Habitat loss

One of the main reasons some bats are endangered is **habitat loss**. Habitat loss is the destruction of the natural areas in which animals live and find food. One way people cause habitat loss is by **clearing** forests.

People clear forests to get wood for **lumber** and to make room to plant crops. They also clear land to build houses and roads.

The Marianas flying fox (above) is endangered because of habitat loss. The tropical forests in which this species lives are being cleared.

Extra caution required

Some bat species live only in certain areas on Earth. For example, many bat species live only in rain forests. Some of those species may live only in a small part of one rain forest! Bats that live only in one area of Earth are at high risk of becoming endangered if their habitat is changed. Other bats live in larger areas, but they feed only on certain kinds of plants. If the plants they eat are destroyed, these bats may also become endangered.

The Madagascar flying fox lives only in Madagascar. The population of Madagascar flying foxes is decreasing due to habitat loss. When trees are cut down, these bats have nowhere to form their camps and have difficulty finding food.

Pesticides and pollution

Farmers around the world use **pesticides**, or harmful chemicals that poison and kill insects. Farmers spray crops of fruits and vegetables, as well as other plants, with pesticides to kill the insects that eat these plants. By using pesticides, farmers put bats at risk, however.

When bats eat poisoned insects, they are poisoned as well. Species such as big brown bats may someday become endangered if too many of them die from eating poisoned insects.

Gray bats are endangered. They often eat insects that have been poisoned by pesticides.

No polluting!

People also **pollute** bat habitats. To pollute an area means to add garbage or chemicals to it. Polluting an area harms the plants and animals that live in that area. When people pollute the areas in which bats live, bats may become sick or die.

The greater bulldog bat eats fish. If people pollute streams and rivers, the fish may die. As a result, the greater bulldog bat will not have any food to eat.

People sometimes spray harmful chemicals in their attics and basements to kill insects. When bats roost in these places, they can get sick by perching on the areas that have been sprayed with the chemicals. These greater mouse-eared bats may be in danger of being poisoned!

25

Do not disturb!

Many species of bats are endangered because people disturb their hibernacula. When people find bats hibernating in attics or in basements, they often force the bats outside or kill them.

Cave explorers

Groups of people often visit caves where bats hibernate. Many do not realize that visiting bat habitats while the animals are hibernating can kill the bats. The glare of flashlights, loud noises, and even people walking through the caves can wake bats out of their deep sleeps. When the bats are disturbed, they fly around looking for food and use up their stored energy. The bats can seldom find enough food in winter, and many starve.

Indiana bats

Indiana bats live in the eastern United States. These bats need to hibernate in cool, moist hibernacula to survive winter. There are only a few caves and mines in the area that provide these conditions, however. As a result, many colonies of Indiana bats must hibernate together in each hibernaculum. If even one of the hibernacula is disturbed by people, thousands of Indiana bats may die at once.

Working to save bats

Conservationists are people who work to protect animals and their habitats. In temperate areas, conservationists try to protect bat hibernacula. One way they protect bats is by stopping people from entering caves and mines that contain hibernacula.

Conservationists put gates in front of the entrances to mines and caves that people no longer use. In some places, they also put up **artificial**, or human-made, perches on cave walls. Artificial perches provide more places from which bats can hang during hibernation.

Gates allow bats to fly in and out of caves, but they prevent people from entering the caves.

Buildings for bats

Conservationists believe that people can help raise bat populations by building homes for bats. **Bat houses** are artificial roosts that provide bats with safe places to live.

Studying to save

Many scientists study bats in the wild or in zoos. They learn about bat migration routes, where bats hibernate, and how they raise their pups. By studying bats, scientists learn what bats need to survive and how to protect them. When scientists share this information with others, more people can learn about bats and keep them from becoming endangered.

The scientist on the right is telling kids about ways they can help bats.

a human-made bat house

Bat watching

You can learn more about bats by watching them in action. Although people entering caves and other hibernacula is unsafe for bats, there are ways that you can see these amazing animals without harming them. In some areas, there are local bat-watching groups that you can join. You can also create a bat-watching group with your friends and family.

Wait and see

The best place to watch bats is near a lake or a stream at the edge of a forest. From this location, you might see bats flying among the trees or **skimming** the water to eat insects. If there are no bats near your home, you can go to a zoo to see several species of bats. Pay attention to what the bats are doing. Are they flying high up in the trees or low to the ground? Are they twisting and turning? Write down or draw what you see so that you have a record of your bat sightings to share with others.

Learn more!

You can learn more about bats and how people
are helping them by checking out these websites:

- **www.batcon.org**
  Read what Bat Conservation International is doing to
  save endangered bats and increase their populations.
- **www.batconservation.org/content/Kidsandbats.html**
  Test what you have learned by taking a quiz about bats.
  You can also learn the proper way to build a bat house!
- **www.fws.gov/endangered/bats/bats.htm**
  The U.S. Fish & Wildlife Service website is an
  excellent source for bat information. Learn about the
  bats that are endangered in the area where you live.

Glossary

Note: Boldfaced words that are defined in the text may not appear in the glossary.

backbone A row of bones in the middle of an animal's back

clearing Removing all the trees and other plants from an area to make it available for use by people

continent One of the seven large areas of land on Earth (Africa, Antarctica, Asia, Australia, Europe, North America, and South America)

crops Plants grown by people for food

domestic Describing animals that are raised by humans as livestock or as pets

hibernaculum A winter roost where some bats hibernate

lumber Boards cut from logs

mine An artificial underground area where people work to find minerals such as gold

population The total number of one type of animal living in a certain area

predator An animal that hunts and eats other animals

pregnant Describing a female animal that has one or more babies growing inside her

skimming Flying along the surface of something, such as land or water

widespread Describing something that can be found over a large area

wingspan The length across the wings of a flying animal, from wingtip to wingtip

Index

1 2 3 4 5 6 7 8 9 0   Printed in the U.S.A.   5 4 3 2 1 0 9 8 7 6